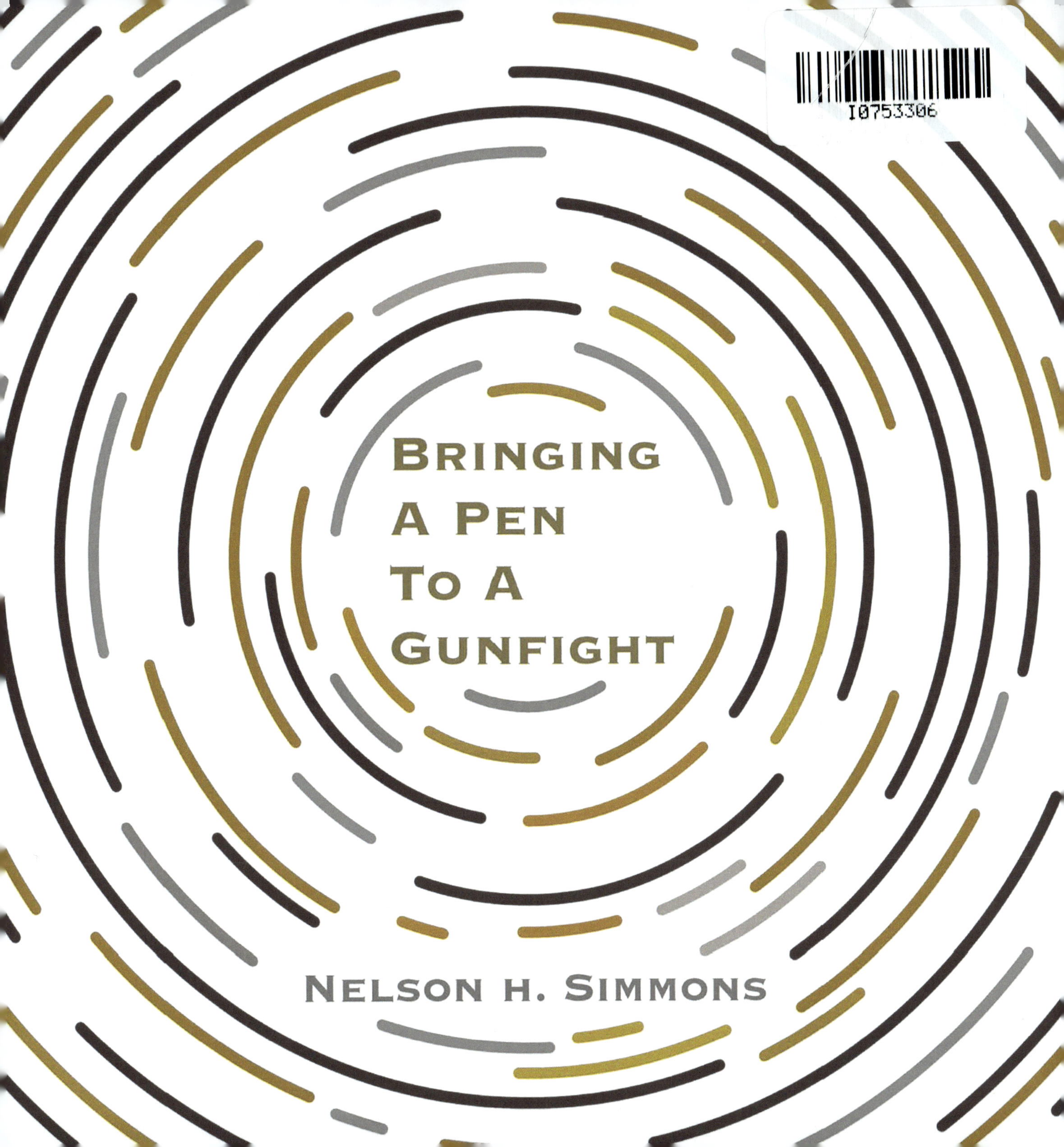
I0753306
Bringing
A Pen
To A
Gunfight
Nelson H. Simmons

Bringing A Pen To A Gunfight

ISBN 979-8-9850995-2-2

Self-published by Nelson H. Simmons and affiliated partners
Contact the author at traciwrites@storyboardstars.com

Bringing A Pen To A Gunfight

Nelson H. Simmons

Dedication

This book is dedicated to family. On my mother's side, Sallie Carter, an embodiment of perseverance, action, and success. She started a family that became and still is becoming a beautiful and fruitful group of people whose hearts are filled with talent, joy, wisdom, and love. For that, I thank her. On my father's side, a tightly-knit group of people who love to laugh, smile, and provide everytime they're together. They have always provided great support and even greater memories that fill me with happiness. For that, I thank them.

Foreword

Grammy Award winning gospel artist, Tasha Cobbs-Leonard in a television interview with, Jennifer Hudson, a fellow Grammy Award winner and R&B artist, talked about how she comes from a family of singers. "I actually was not the *chosen* vocalist," she said. "I have cousins who can just--whooo!" What Mrs. Cobbs-Leonard was conveying in her statement is that while she is the one who wound up cutting the record deal and, rightfully so, becoming famous, there are several others in her family who can absolutely *out-sing* her.

How many tales of the same might we recall throughout our own lives? Most people have encountered someone with a particular gift or talent enabling them to produce a certain something which far exceeds the quality of that which is greatly renowned.

The young man whose writings you are about to experience is one such example. Like his mother, this young man loves words; and he garners as much self-satisfaction from releasing and constructing the flood of ideas inside of his head as he does from drawing a reaction from his readers.

Partake in this book of raw artistry because it is authentic, creative, and downright interesting. The photographs are the product of a kid who knew nothing about digital photography, took a class, loved it, and made the places he visited his muse. The poems – some for fun, some from passion, some for purpose, are the product of no other choice...no other choice but to write.

Enjoy,
Traci Simmons
Mother, Author, Writer

Poems

Prologue In Poetry 9

I Come From 11

How Do You...Chicago? 13

U.N.R.E.C.I.P.R.O.C.A.T.E.D. 15

Based On A True Story: Part 1, Community 17

My Thoughts At Night 19

Hide 21

Love Wrote A Waltz 25

I Hope The Ink On This Page Comes To Life 27

Based On A True Story: Part 2, My People 31

Happy Birthday 35

My Typa Day 37

Conclusion 39

Based On A True Story: Part 3, The Cut 41

Canary 45

Photos

SHADOW?

CREATING FLAMES

WHAT'S SO FUNNY?

SUNSETS AND CUT GRASS

A LONG WALK HOME

GOING AWAY

KEEPING THE DOCTOR AWAY

DON'T NEED A CLOVER TO HAVE LUCK

FIRST DAY

INFINITE

THE RED LINE

WELCOME

REACHING OUT

ROAD TRIPS

SUNNY WINTER

BLUEBERRY PIE FOR THE WINTER

RUSTLING ROOTS

MUSICAL MIST

JAZZ BUZZ

POSTCARD FOR A SOCCER GAME

BRANCHES OF A BLOODLINE

COUSINS

TWINS

CLONES

FAMILY TIME

GROWING THROUGH

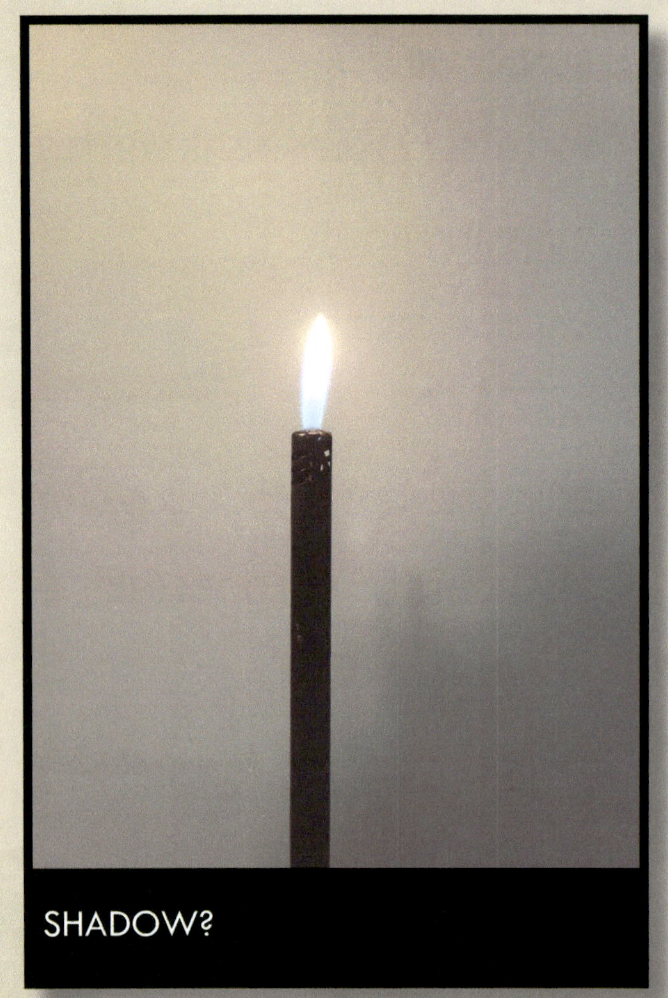

SHADOW?

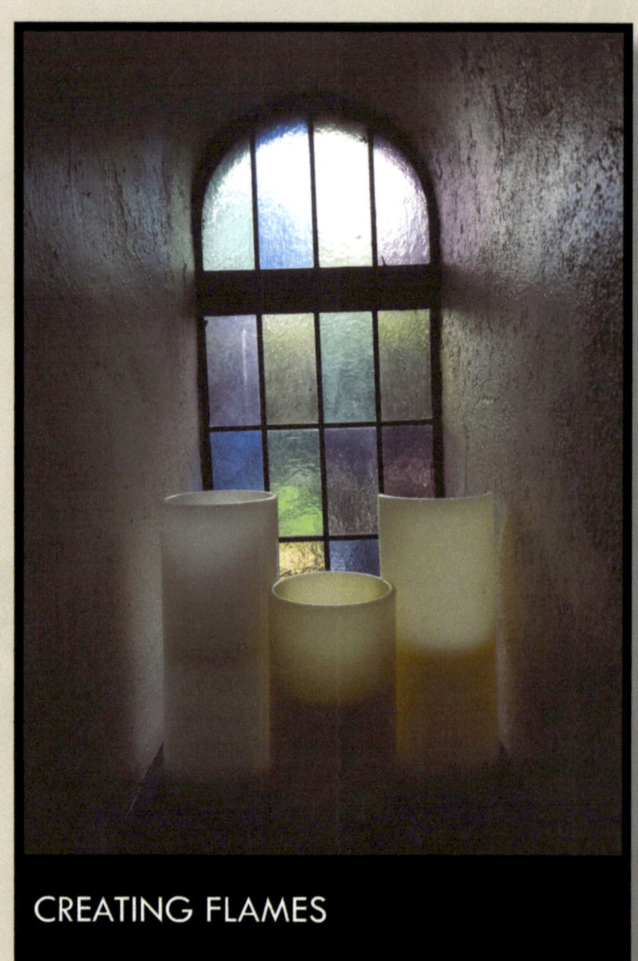

CREATING FLAMES

Prologue In Poetry

I thought of writing a poem called,
"Is Fire Afraid To Burn?"
Because it sounded *poetic*
I started writing and
When I finished,
The page was blank and white, no ink whatsoever

All I saw were,
Sets of jumbles of letters,
Stacked on top of one another,
Laying there, unmoving,
Like corpses.

I was flustered, asking myself,
"Why aren't my words alive?"
I thought my vision was going bad so I went to clean my glasses.
I put them back on and,
These words were still lying there,
Unmoving,
Like corpses.

See, my poem, my words, my story,
They were not leaping and bounding all over the room.
They weren't dragging me through a literary portal,
Into a dimension of my own words,
Like they normally do.

And I, again, wondered,
"Why?"

After a few minutes of pondering this,
I came to the conclusion that is as follows:
What is poetry, without depth?
Nothing.

Luckily,
These following poems are not,
Nothing...

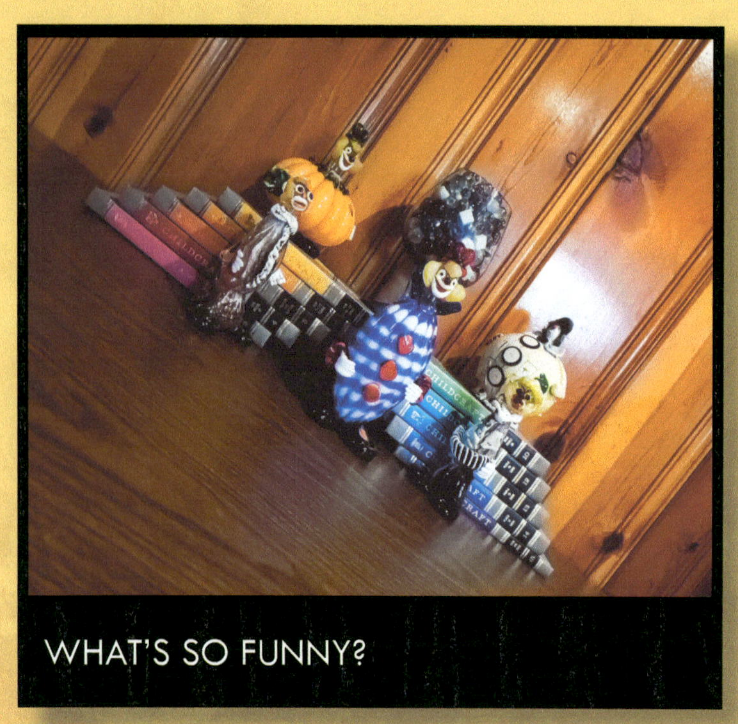

WHAT'S SO FUNNY?

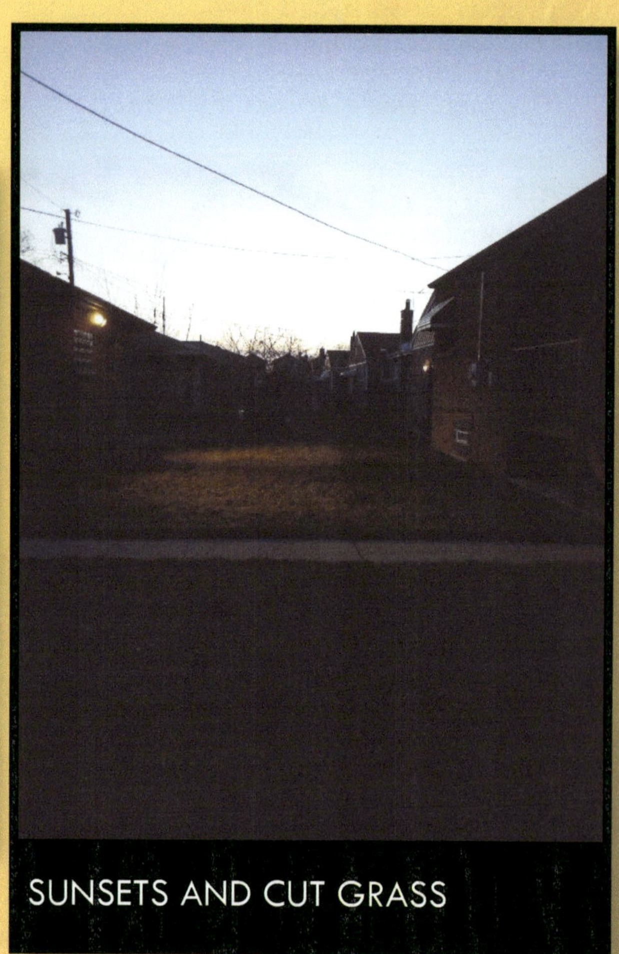

SUNSETS AND CUT GRASS

I Come From

I come from the depths of Chatham,
With graffiti on the crumbling brick buildings.
And bleak blackness weaving itself into the potential of blackness, bright.
From riding my bike in the muddy waters after rainy days cuz I had nothing else to do,
And gunshots and car-jackings and police sirens and ambulances and thugs and,
Fear.
That remind me how much I despise the depths of Chatham.

I come from a wooden container,
Trapped inside of it are my achievements in oratory.
And sitting on Her couch, discussing grades.
From eating my ve-ge-ta-bles
That are somehow sweet, although the ingredients are not.
I come from running into the basement of Her house with my brother.
From, my aunt who shared an abode with Rosa Parks......
I come from Rosa Parks, who shared an abode with my aunt.
And from, Sallie Carter,
My great-great-great grandmother,
A freed slave who founded a school and a church,
And from my grandma, a schoolteacher,
Who, when she was a student, used to get peppers and tomatoes thrown at her while
They called her slurs.
Somehow, she still has a smile on her face
Their determination,
Their passion,
Show me that
My melanin is magnificent!

I come from Thanksgiving dinner with family and,
New Year's fish fry's.
From chasing my cousin at my grandparent's house with a Dora the Explorer toy.
And believing that a shadow monster would get me if I didn't make it to my room in
time after turning off the lights.
They make me realize how much I love the depths of Chatham.

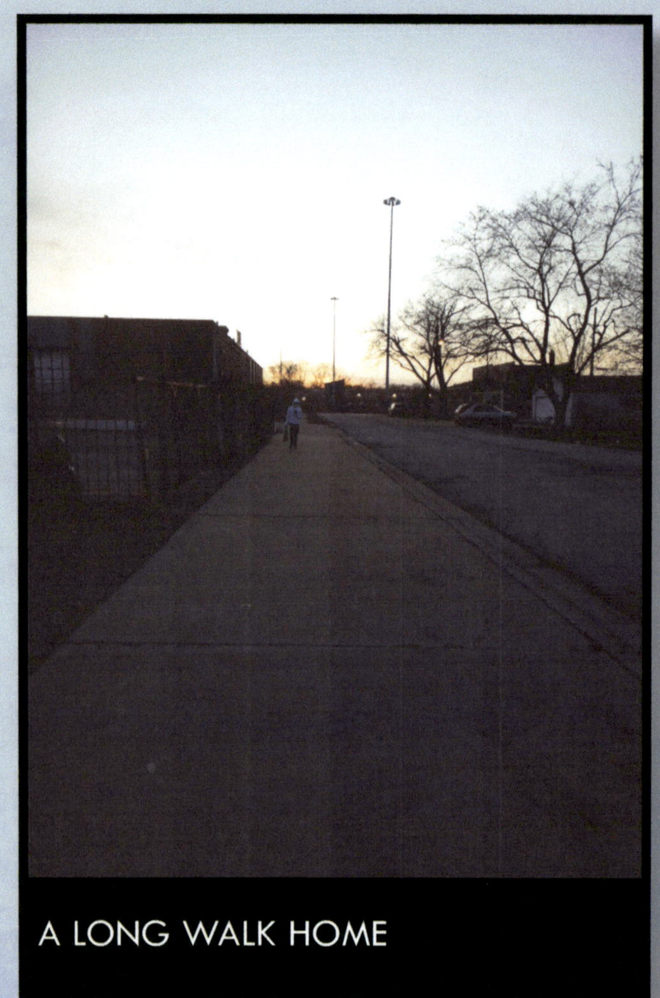

A LONG WALK HOME

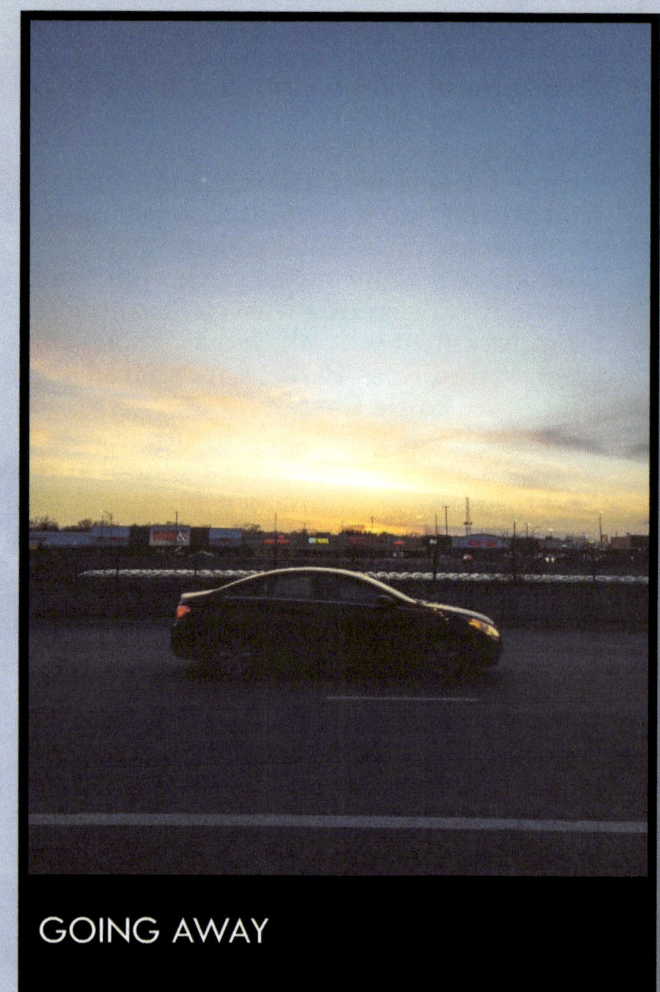

GOING AWAY

How Do You...Chicago?

Dear Chicago,

Are You a place?
Are You a people?
Are You the music?
Are You the food?
Are You the Cubs or the White Sox?

Are You a hope? Are You a love?
Are You a despair? Are You run down?
Are You divided? Are You peaceful?
Are You bullets? Are You many?
Are You void? Are You family?

How do You manage to be all of these?
How do You manage to make the jazz of the sax match the thunder of the CTA?
How do You make the vibrant graffiti match the colors of the people?

How do You...Chicago?
How do You...Chicago?
......
You are,
You do,
Chicago.

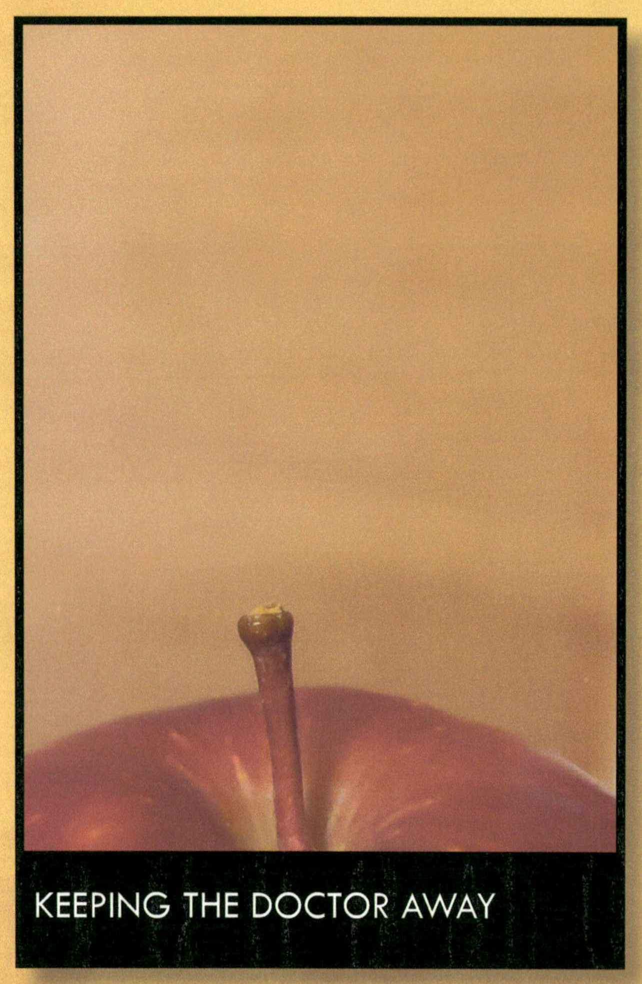

KEEPING THE DOCTOR AWAY

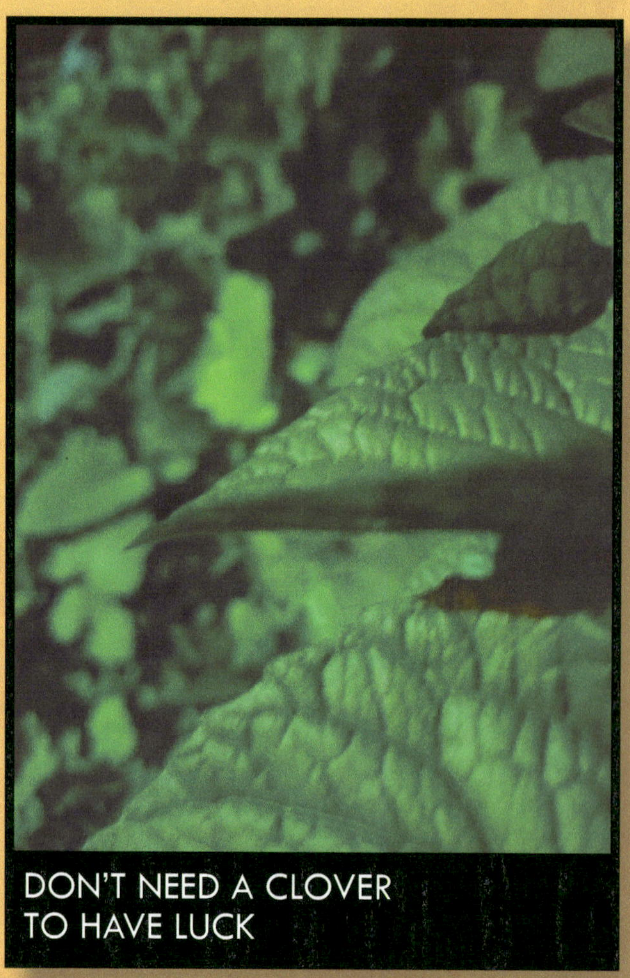

DON'T NEED A CLOVER
TO HAVE LUCK

U.N.R.E.C.I.P.R.O.C.A.T.E.D.

Underneath the stars,
Pondering the "what-ifs."
I am
Never to speak again
So, I write.
I am
Running away,
But struggling to.
I am
Enduring the hurt of
"No."
I am
Chasing realities;
They seem more of fantasies.
I am
Itching to break the silence
That Fear keeps intact.
I am
Playing potential, but parting possibilities,
And replaying them in my head.
I am
Remembering how full I was;
Reflecting on how void I am.
I am
Obviously breaking; Openly thinking. But,
Overly anticipating something that's not there.
I am
Crashing and burning; Actively learning
From my mistakes... and my suffering.
I am
Awaiting the tomorrow after infinite tomorrows
When this all blows over.
I am
Tearing myself apart,
Piece by piece until only my heartless heart remains.
I am
Ever so slightly
Fading away, along with my hope.
I am
Done.

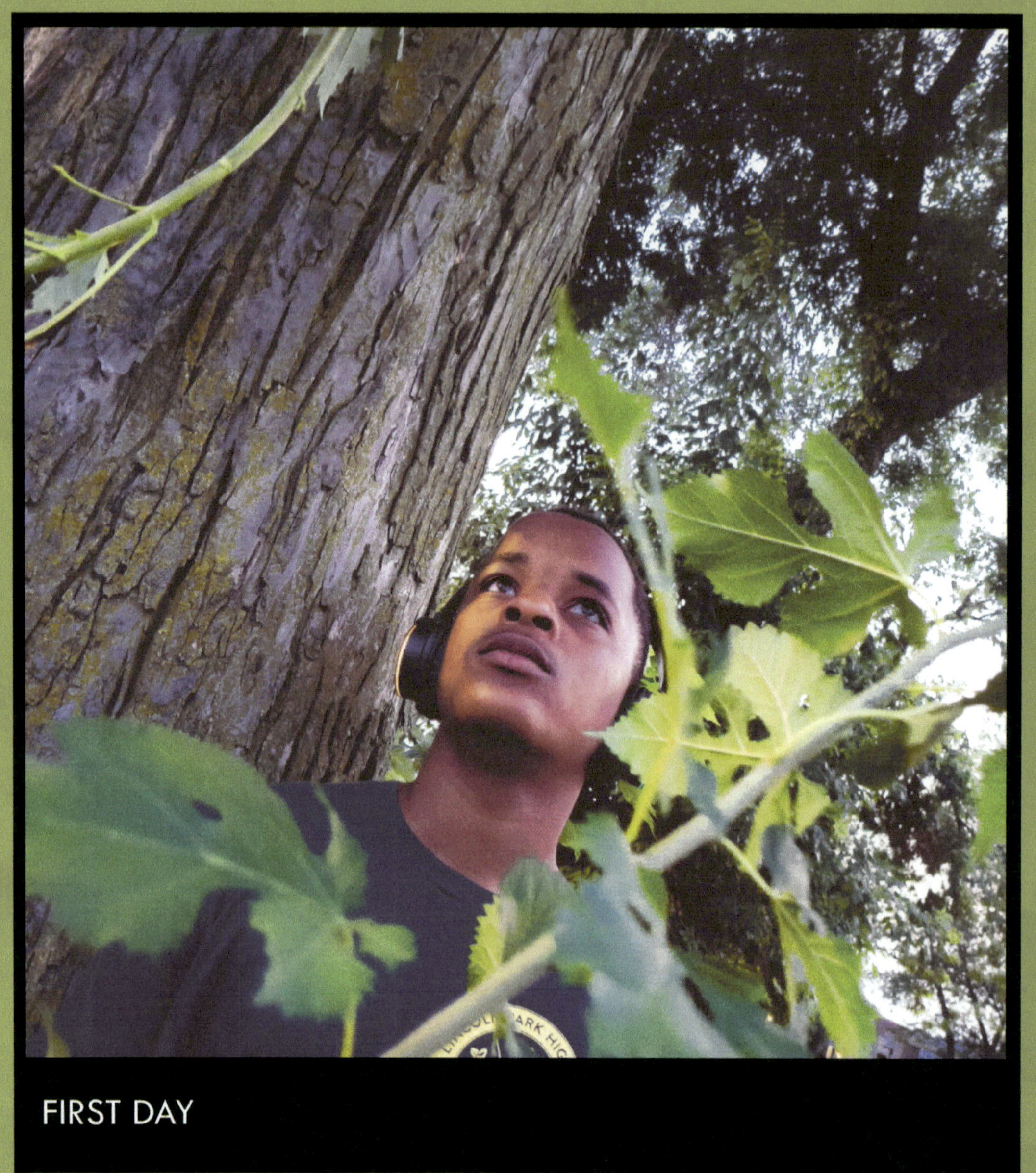

FIRST DAY

Based On A True Story: Part 1, Community

When I walk into the barbershop, I'm a person.
When I sit in the chair, I'm a piece of marble waiting to be carved.

I get out the car.
I walk up to the door.
I get buzzed in.
The first thing I see is a checkered floor.
There's nothing particularly special about this specific checkered floor.
Because, every barbershop has a checkered floor.

There's already someone in the sculptor's chair.
So, I wait.
I listen to the men, some old, some young, but all men.
I listen to the men discuss the current state of music,
And the weather,
And the Bulls game last night.
See, the barbershop is a place where men get to talk and laugh.
And, to get a haircut.

Now, it's very important to get a cut.
Of course it is.
But, if the men ain't talking
You ain't in a barbershop.
Another thing about barbershops,
You won't ever hear a curse word.
Not one.
The people in the barbershop respect clean language.

Sometimes, they'll get caught up in the conversation,
they forget they're getting a haircut.
And even if you're done and even if you've paid,
You can still stay
And you can still talk.
That's the thing about the barbershop.
You won't ever find people not talking.

So next time you get a cut,
Listen to the talking,
And the laughing,
Listen.

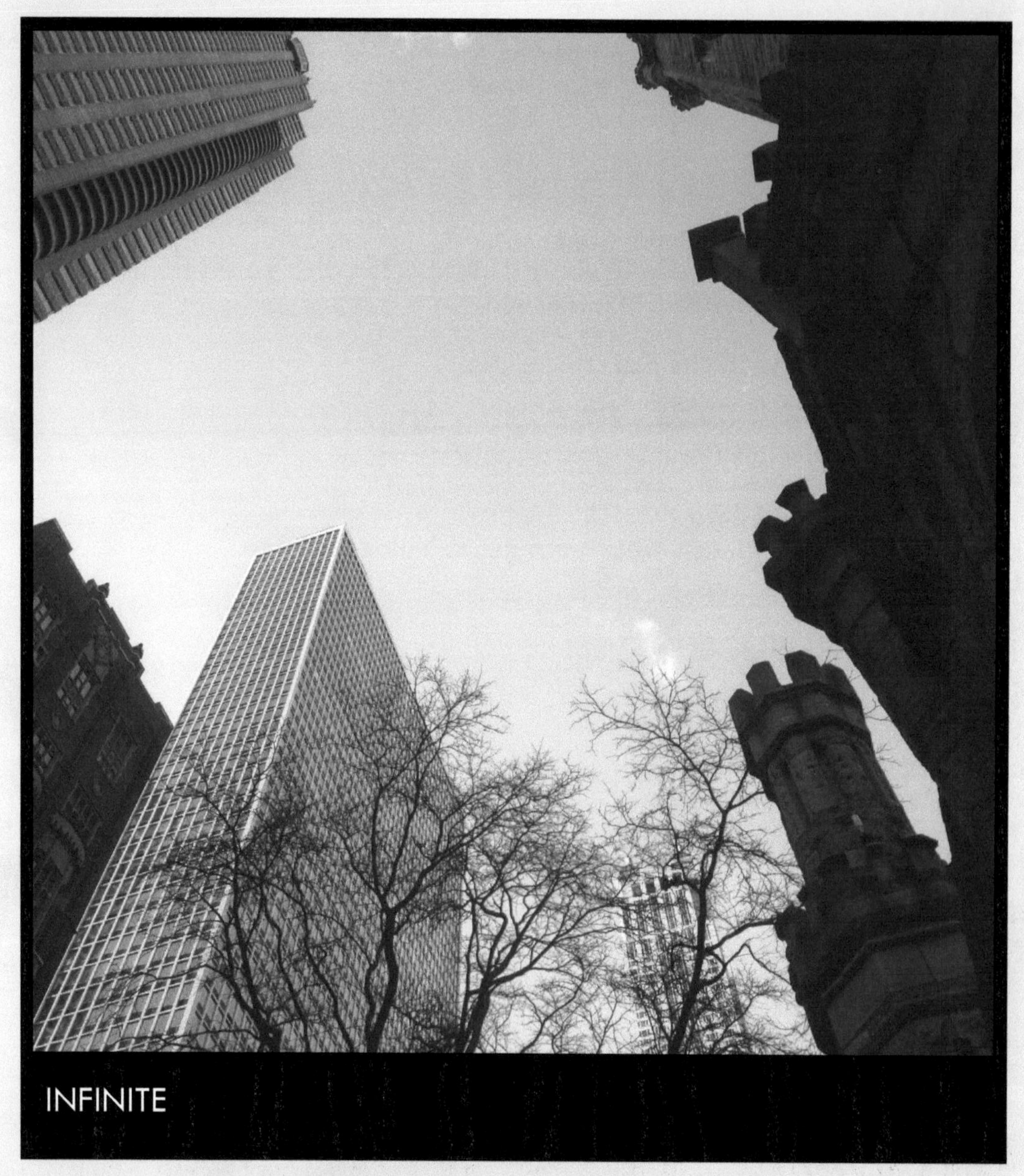

INFINITE

My Thoughts At Night

I need to workout.
Thank you for being there.
I hope I finished my homework.
Is my phone charging?
She's cute.
I need to listen more in World Studies.
Life is good.
I'm so thankful for my friends.
I like ice cream,
I'm happy.
I need to go to sleep cuz I wake up at 5:50 AM.
That's such a good song.
What time is it?
MARVEL is sooooo goooooddddd!
It's Grandma's birthday tomorrow!
I love my friends.
I really need to workout.
Oh shoot!
I have to memorize this monologue soon.
I should hang out with my friends soon. They're so cool bro.
I haven't watched TV in so long.
Remember Quarantine? Oof.
I say "Oof" alot.
Thanks, again.
Guitar is fun.
I miss acting.
I wake up at 5:50 AM. GO TO SLEEP!!!
People are so interesting. Like, HOW is every single person living a different life, all at the same time?!?!?
My 4th Grade teacher was so nice.
I need to write a poem soon.
How happy would I be if I didn't meet you?
I need to go to sleep.
...
Okay,
Goodnight.

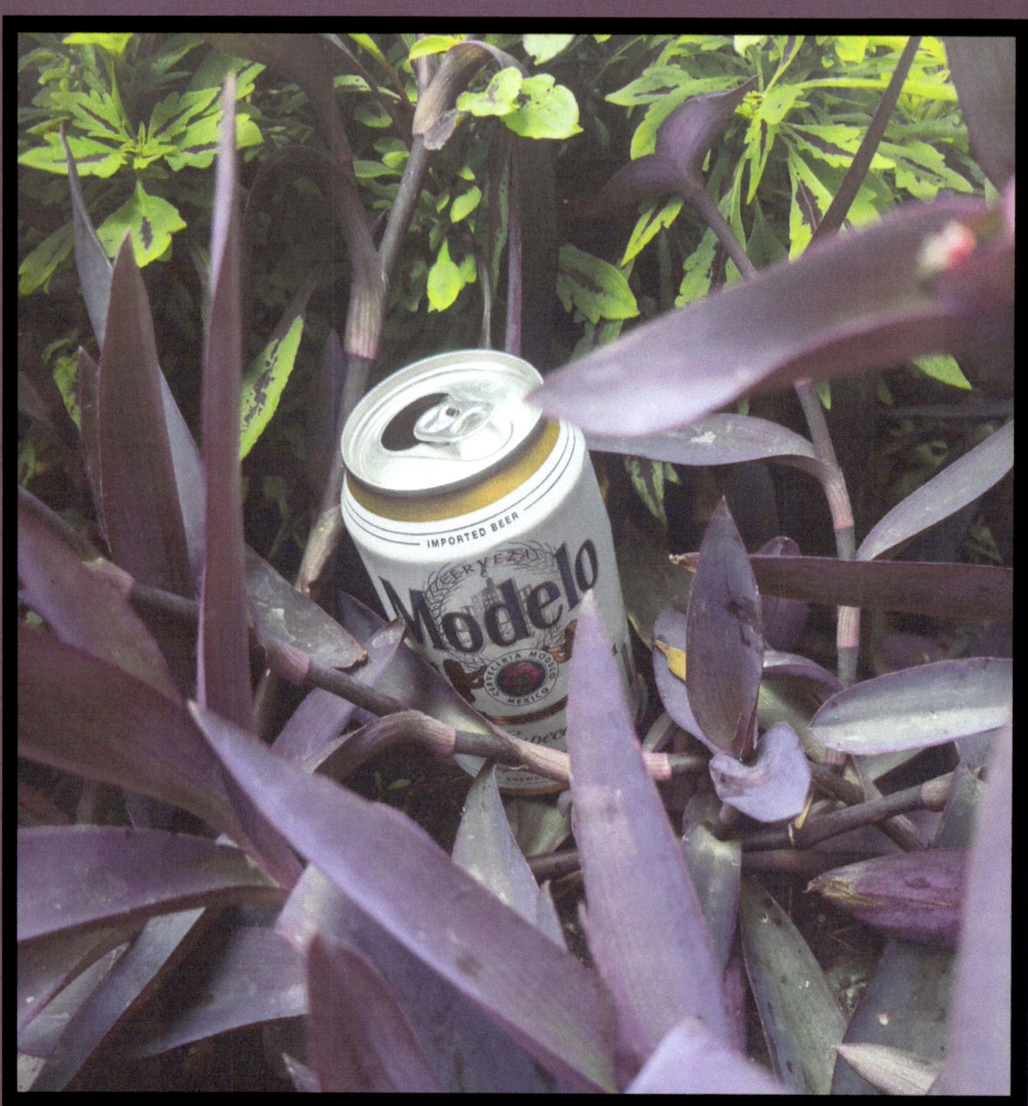

THE RED LINE

Hide

Learning.
Learning in Class.
Learning in Math Class.

Instant Bullets.

SCREAMING ~~STUDENTS~~ VICTIMS

- ▶ Lock the door.
- ▶ Turn off the lights.
- ▶ Hide in the corner.
- ▶ Don't make a sound.

"He was wearing all black."

S o m e.
A r e.
D e a d.

Grieving
Mother

LOUD GUNSHOTS

S I L E N T s i s t e r.

Confused
Friends.

quiet chaos.

b L o O d Y
B o D i E s .

• Police Sirens
• Police Cars
• Police Enter School
• Standing
• Standing
• Standing
• Standing

• Meanwhile, more **LOUD GUNSHOTS** and
quiet chaos and S o m e A r e D y i n g and TEARS NOT DRYING and

b L o O d Y B o D i E s .

• Standing
• Standing
• Standing
• Standing
• Still Standing

NEWS REPORT:
BREAKING:
ONE TEACHER AND NINE STUDENTS.
IN THE THIRD GRADE.

therapy.
empty.

LOCKDOWN FOR A FEW 3.5 HOURS

"We pride ourselves on keeping the students here safe!"
"Safety is our #1 priority!"
"We promise to keep your kids safe!"

missing.

Kids turned into a **HASHTAG** and a **SOCIAL MEDIA POST**.

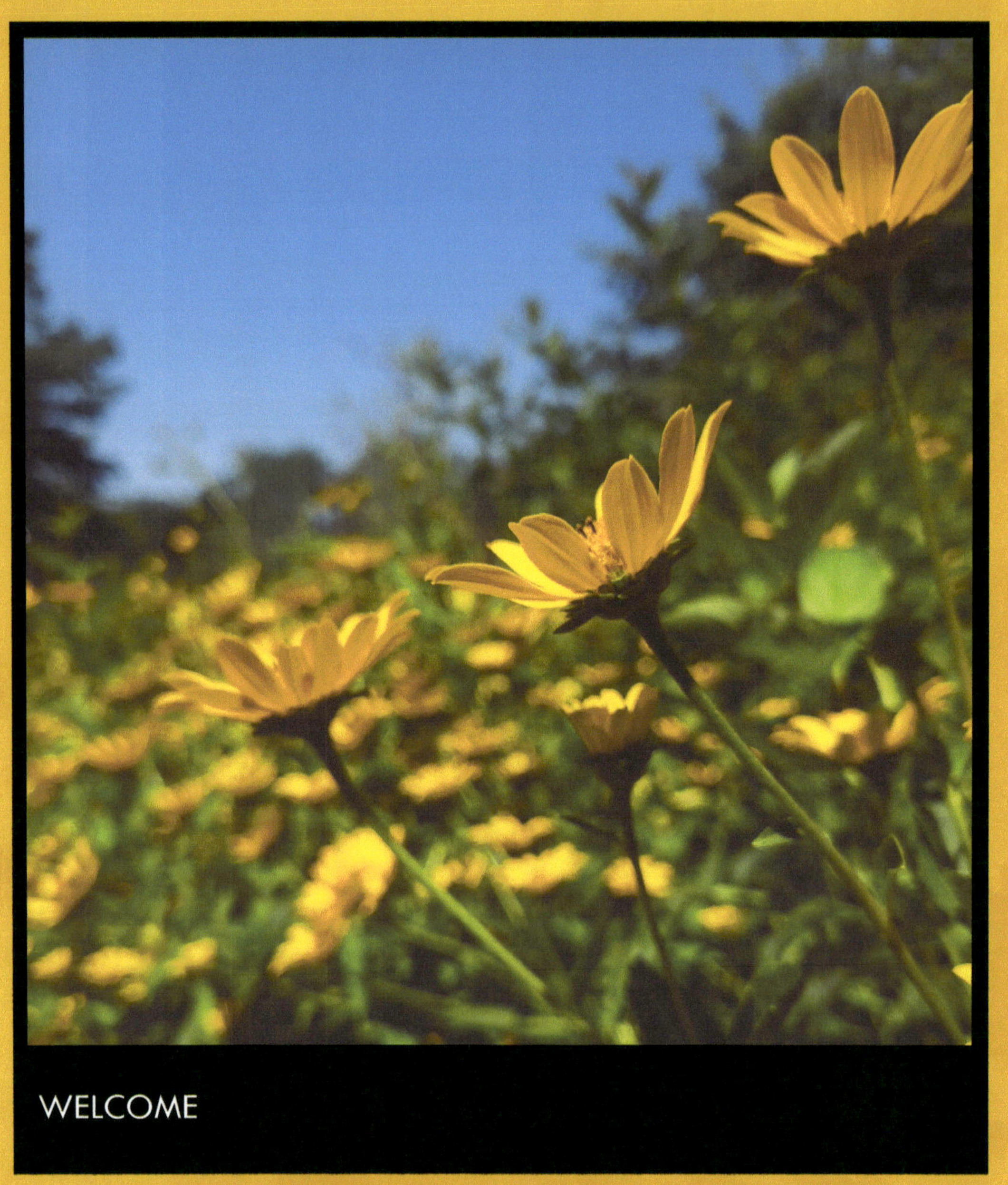
WELCOME

Love Wrote A Waltz

Love wrote a waltz.
Conducted as a concord of desire,
A desire too heavy for any man to bear holding.
Played as a strong stringed symphony,
Not even a sparrow can attempt to sing.

The timpani are the pounding of two hearts,
Yearning to dance with one another.
It has a rhythm that is synchronized with sudden oxytocin spikes.

The bridge, proclaiming the bond between two souls,
Who dance together,
For the first time.

Eros, forging the melodies of love in the heart's raging fire.
Crafted by Hedylogos and Hymenaios.
Beautifully and passionately sung by Pothos.
A masterpiece of Anteros and Aphrodite, finally performed.

Love wrote a waltz.
So may I have this dance?

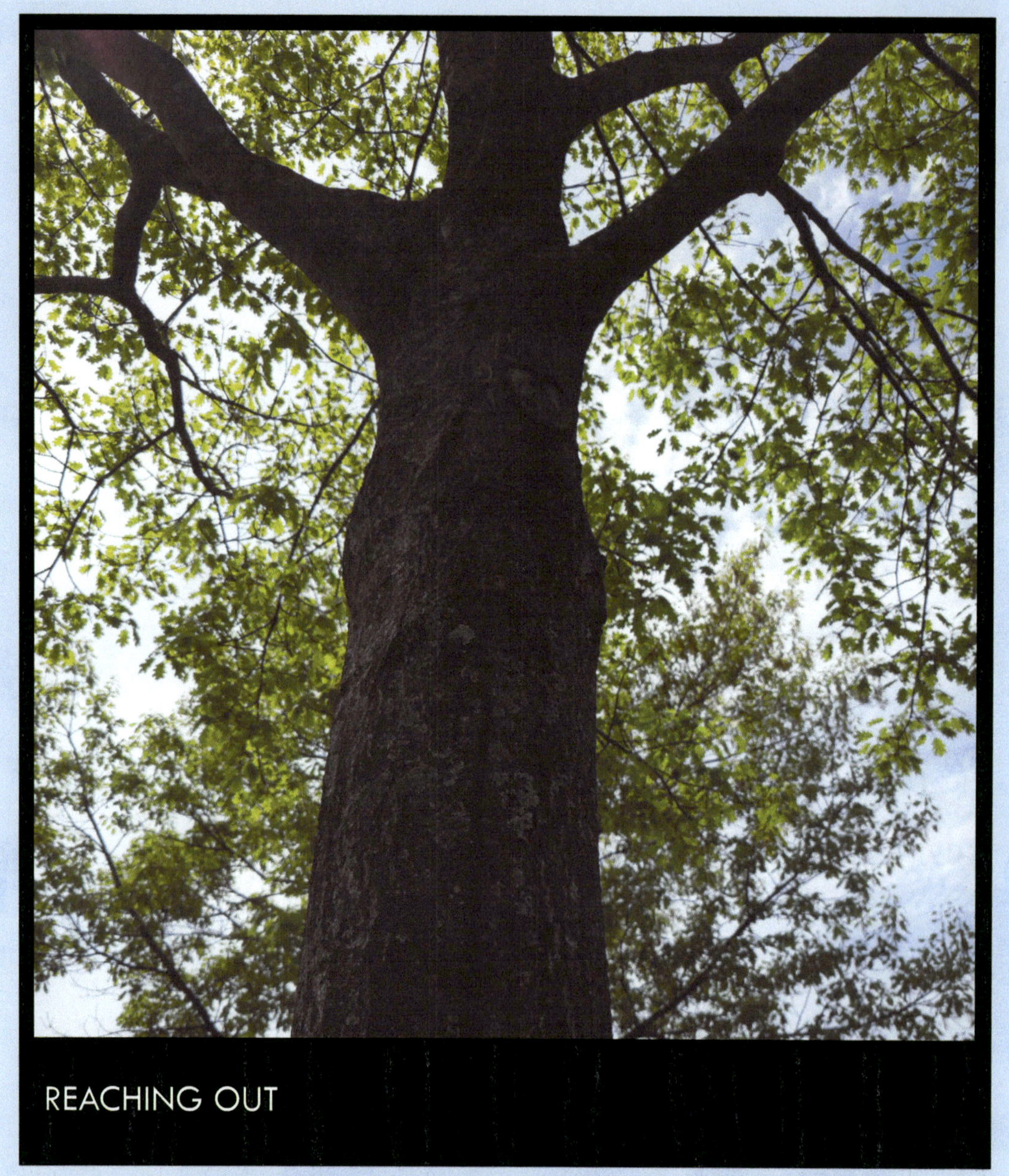

REACHING OUT

I Hope The Ink On This Page Comes To Life

She draws herself; a self-portrait.
But, the girl on the paper is not her.
Because the girl on the paper,
Smiles.

She draws herself with a smile,
In hopes that she could be able to.
She says, through frantic invisible tears,
"The girl on the paper is me.
And the girl on the paper smiles.
So, then I should smile too.
I'm smiling now, see?
That means I'm happy.
See?"

She draws in black and white,
But there is color in her eyes.
I see the red of her pain,
And the green of her self-hate,
And the blue of her sorrow,
And the grey of her despair.
All of this color,
All in her eyes.

She spent so much time acting like she was okay.
And I ask myself,
"Why is she acting in her own life?"

And then I see her tears.
They stream down her face.
And those tears, answer my question.
They tell me, weak,
"We are filled with agony!
Please... help us."
They say,
"She acts happy because she is weighing everyone down."
And I am silent.
...
...

And in a fraction of a second, an urge to scream comes over me.
I want to scream to her,
My heart beats faster,
I want her to know what I feel,

I need her to know what I feel,
I need to tell her,

"You are not a burden to anyone!
You weep, and even your tears cry out for help,
If you could just cry out for help too,
You will find what you need!
And you will find who you need.
And that someone,
Or that something,
I promise,
Will give you what you need.
If you would just cry out!"

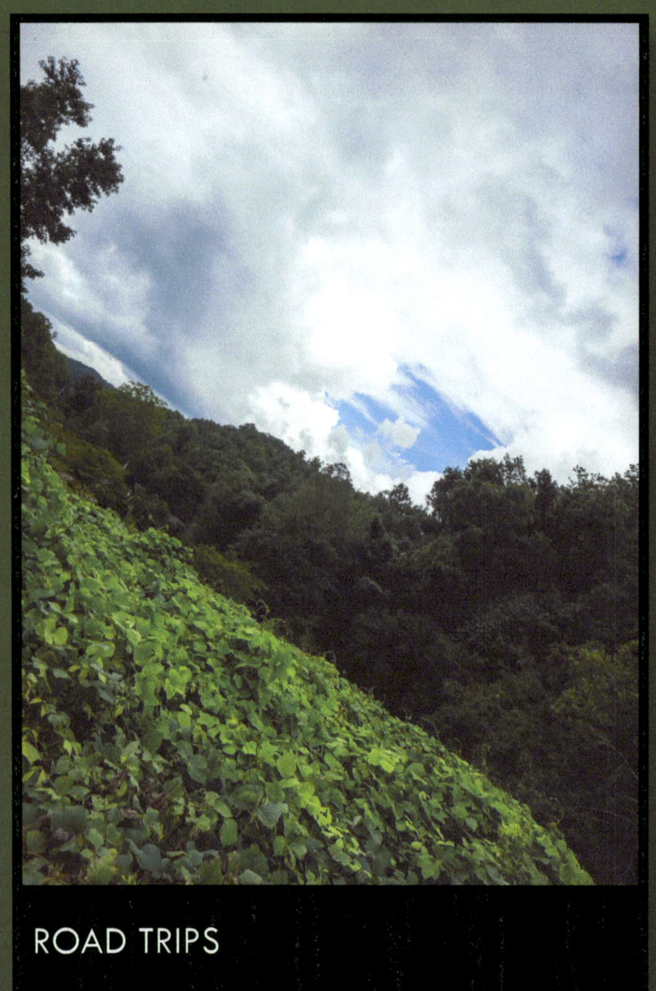

ROAD TRIPS

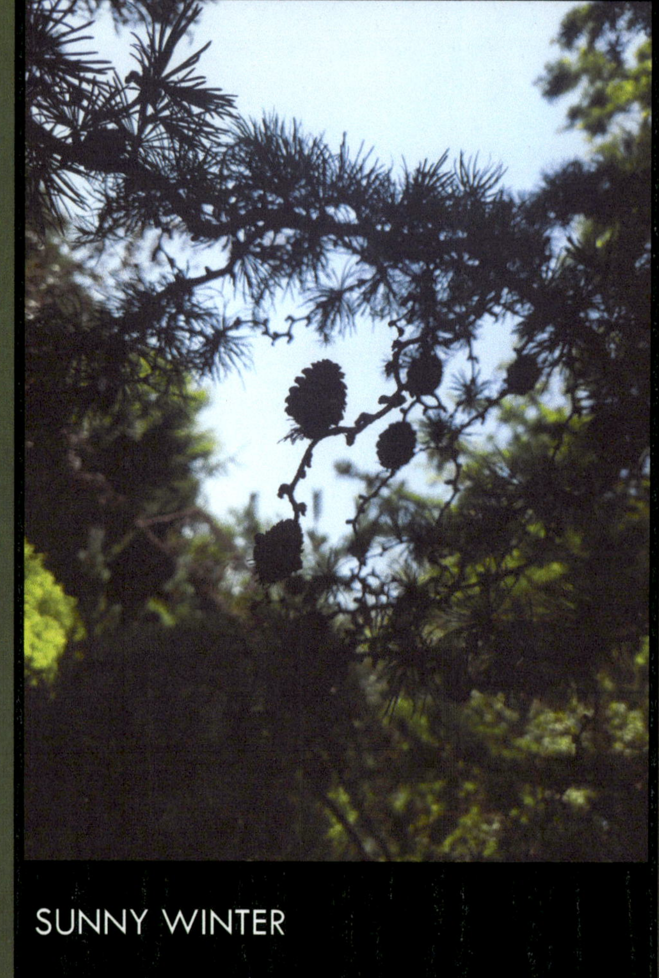

SUNNY WINTER

Based On A True Story: Part 2, My People

When I walk into the barbershop, I'm a person.
When I sit in the chair, I'm a piece of marble waiting to be carved.

I get out the car.
I walk up to the door.
I get buzzed in.
The first thing I see is a checkered floor.
There's nothing particularly special about this specific checkered floor.
Because, every barbershop has a checkered floor

Ever since the dawn of time,
Meaning fifteen years ago,
The barbershops that I've been to have been Black.
All the barbershops in TV shows and movies have been Black.
The people are Black,
The music is Black,
The cuts are Black,
The vibe is Black.

R&B mixed with,
A nice fade,
Mixed with the brown shade,
Mixed with the razor blade,
And the people who stayed,
After they've paid.
If I had to give it a grade,
On the Blackness that's displayed
At my barbershop,
I'd give it a 110%

Whenever I walk into a barbershop,
I see melanin.
I see young melanin, old melanin.
Dark melanin and light melanin.
Loud and soft melanin.
I see energetic melanin,
I see sleeping melanin.
Talking melanin,
Listening melanin.
I see melanin.

And I can't tell you a reason as to why,
Because I don't have much of a clue.
I cannot give you a reason

Except that:
It's my neighborhood.

And
It's my people.

Neither of my parents have gone to a barbershop that wasn't
Black.
It's not a coincidence.
It's our culture.
Black people have been going to the Black barbershops for a long, long time.
And I don't expect that to change.

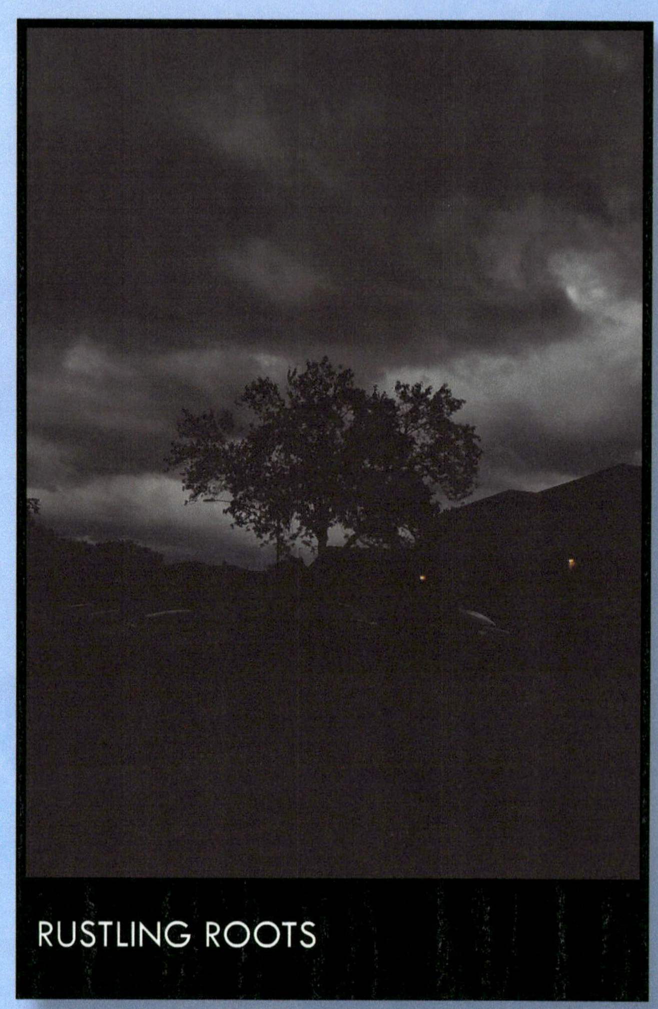

RUSTLING ROOTS

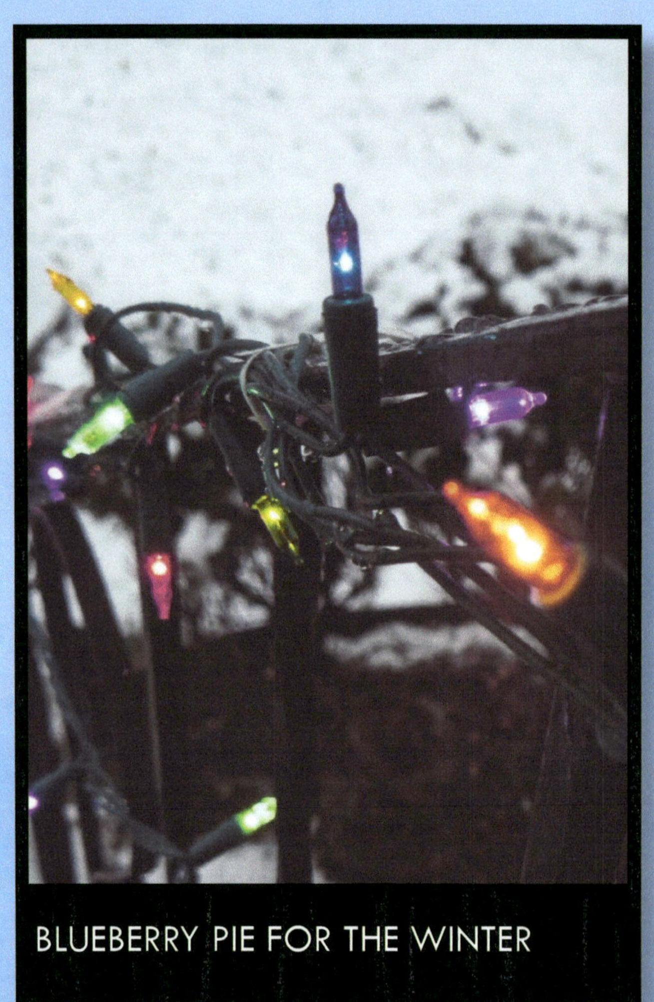

BLUEBERRY PIE FOR THE WINTER

Happy Birthday

Happy Birthday Black Child!
Ya' life means nothing.
See I've set your life up where you can't do nothin' to try and thrive.
And if you strive to climb your way up in life,
Imma. Rip. You. Right. Apart.
See, see your tears are my gasoline.
Your agony, my life support.
Happy Birthday, Black Child!

Happy Birthday Black Boy!
You eighteen now.
Can't call you a boy anymore.
But I sure can sentence you as a man.
Imma have fun with that!
See, see I've been messin' around with you people fo' a loooong time,
Tellin' my guys to go and put bullets in y'all's chests,
Like a game of darts.
And if that don't work, I can tell a jury some ridiculous excuse, "I was fearin' for my life!"
Happy Birthday Black Boy!

Happy Birthday Black Girl!
Oooooohhhh!!!
Imma paint you like I'm Pablo Picasso!
I can use my spray paint to color you like a skank or a stripper or a prostitute.
I'll use my airbrush to stain you like a ghetto talkin' little whore!
I'll mold you as a loud-mouth temperamental slut with my clay.
No one's gon' hire you as a manager now!
I tried my hardest with that Karisha, Kamalia Harris or whatever.
And that Ke-Ketan...Ketanji Brown Jackson slipped through too.
They somehow beat me.
I CAN'T let that happen again with you can I?
Happy Birthday Black Girl!

Happy Birthday,
From your,
Uncle Sam.

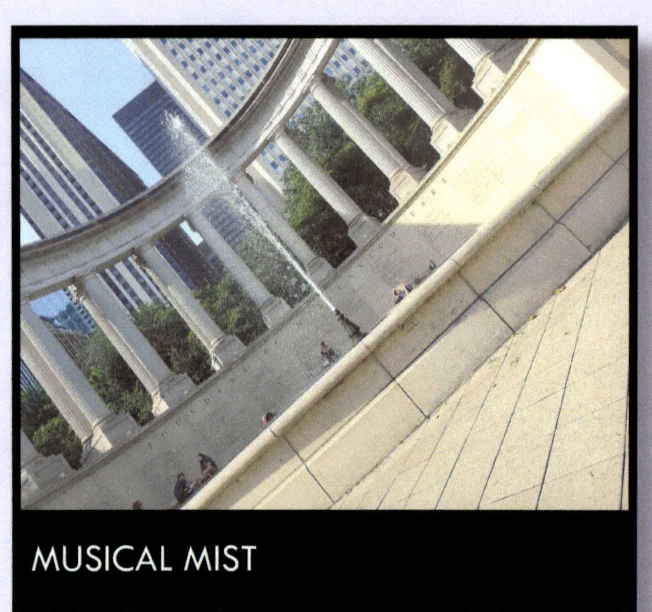

MUSICAL MIST

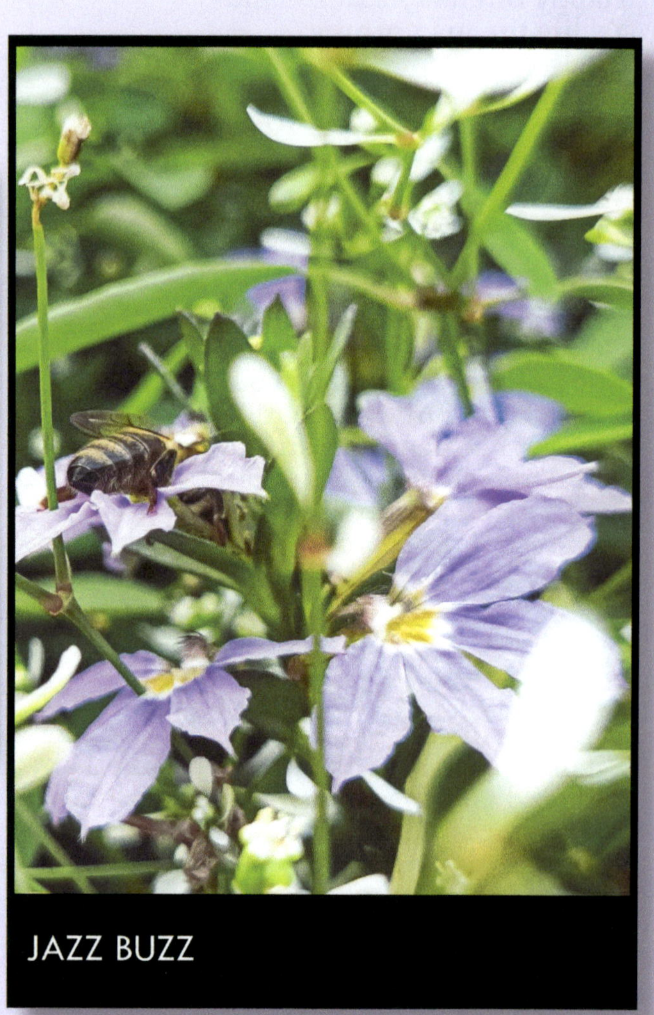

JAZZ BUZZ

My Typa Day

A cool 70, with a crisp summer breeze
Out on the lakeshore,
Walkin' and Talkin' and Laughin'
'Bout life and
Us just being happy
Happy, where we are;

You got:
The Loving One,
The Funny One,
The Quiet One,
I'm The Loud One,
You got:
The Bold One,
The "Parent",
The Picture One,
The Video One, and
The Like-A-Brother or a Sister One;
All clicking together,
Like pieces of a puzzle.

Oooohhhh,
We just havin' a grand ole time!
Runnin' back and forth,
Making jokes,
Surrounded by strangers,
Strangers just watchin' some kids mess around,
Strangers on our left that look down on us with disgust,
Strangers on our right that just smile, remembering when they did the same thing,
But what I see when I look around,
Is, the people I love,
Cuz, when I focus on the fun and the friendship,
Those strangers seem to slip away,
Into tiny little particles of the air,
All their conversations,
Merge with the crashing of the waves,
And the squawking of the seagulls.

See, this,
This is my typa day

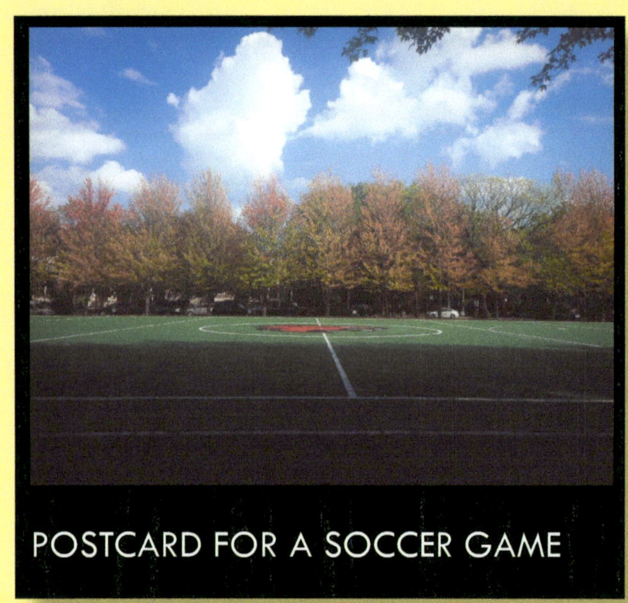

POSTCARD FOR A SOCCER GAME

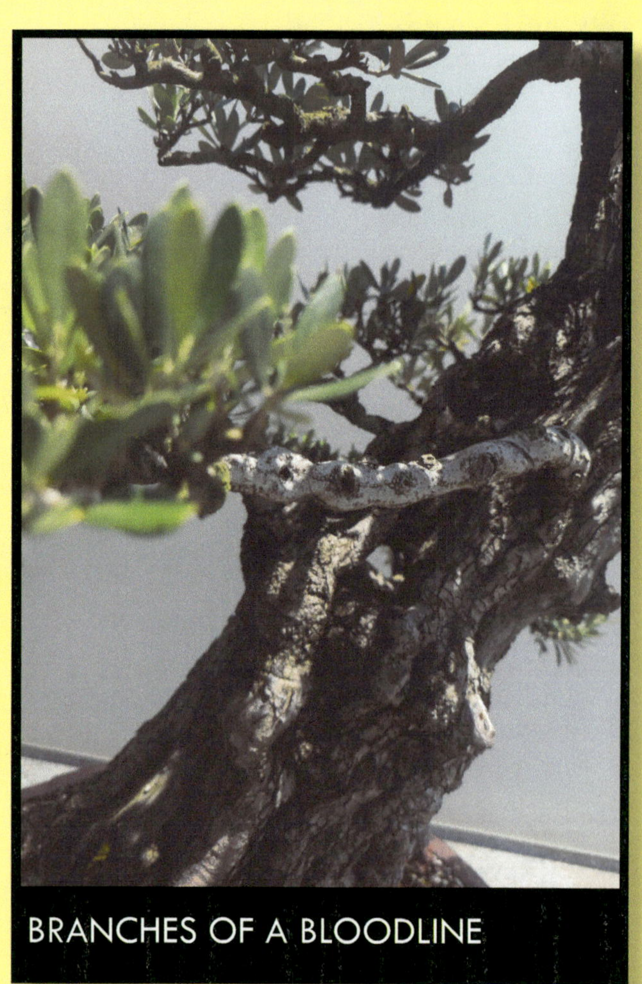

BRANCHES OF A BLOODLINE

Conclusion

The sun rises, and the sun sets. It's just a matter of when.
It's just a matter of if you watch the sun set...

Although you're leaving,
Please still think of me,
I'll just be right here,
Waiting for you,
I pray you're waiting,
For my return, dear,
And every night I'll be dreaming of you.

When you are dismal,
While I am weeping,
Think of each other,
For love and care,
You're almost gone now,
Please do not leave me,
Left with your heartbeat to bid me

Farewell.

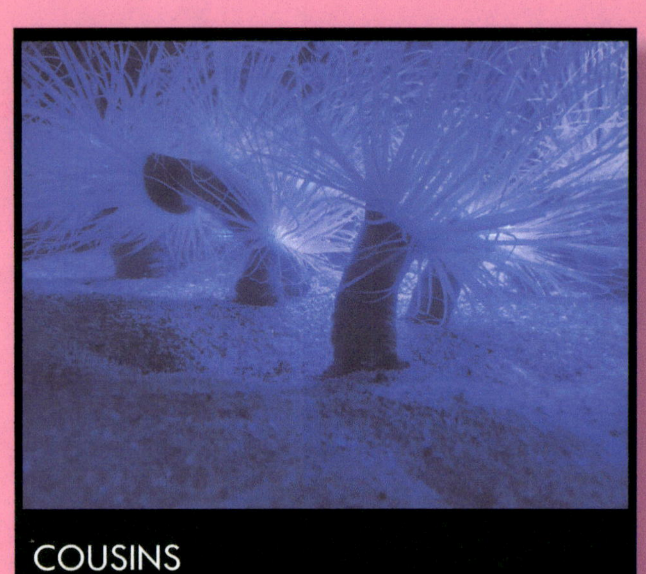

COUSINS

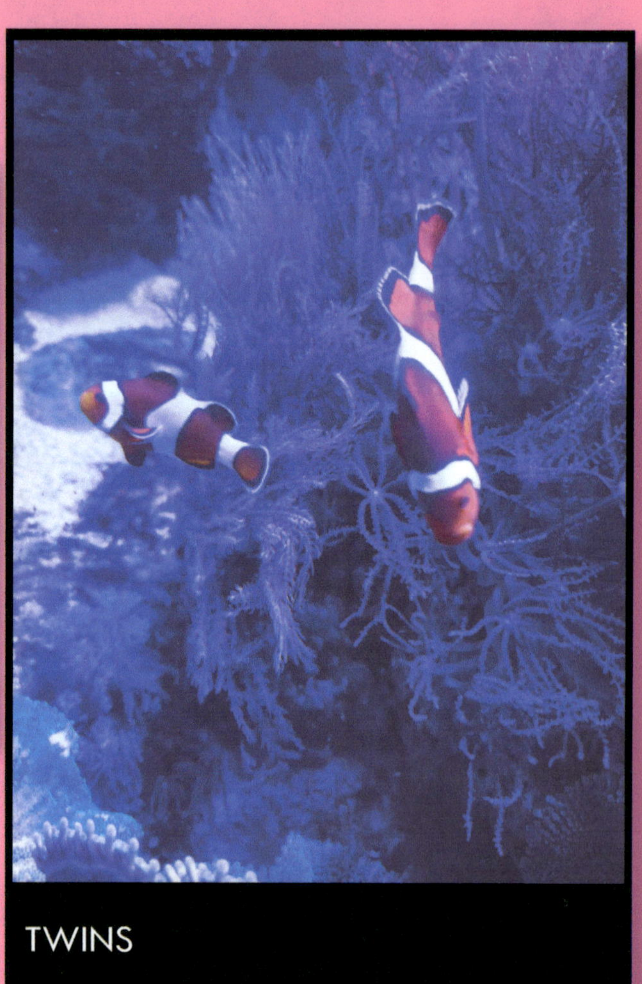

TWINS

Based On A True Story: Part 3, The Cut

When I walk into the barbershop, I'm a person.
When I sit in the chair, I'm a piece of marble waiting to be carved.

I get out the car.
I walk up to the door.
I get buzzed in.
The first thing I see is a checkered floor.
There's nothing particularly special about this specific checkered floor.
Because, every barbershop has a checkered floor.

I used to hate the feeling of not knowing what kind of haircut I wanted.
But now I don't have to worry about that.
I know exactly what I want every time I sit in that chair.
The feeling of the chair's soft leather is magical on your body.
Maybe it's because of the combination of the AC, the chair, and the barber's gown.
Or maybe it's the confidence I have in the barber because I know
He'll make me look clean.

I used to hate the scratchy feeling of that paper-like strip the barber put on my neck.
It scratched my skin and I never understood the reason of it.
He would use the scratchy paper-like strip and
wet it with some alcohol after he was done with the cut.
I used to hate the feeling of that alcohol stinging my upper neck as the barber dabbed it on.
See, I've learned though,
Whenever I feel that,
I know I'm looking good.

In fact, I walk out of that barbershop feelin' myself
Everytime.
I look in the rearview mirror on my way riding home.
I put my headphones on upside-down in fear that I may mess up my new crisp haircut.
I protect my fade.
And don't even get me started on sponging my hair.
Or the pride I feel when someone says,
"Did you get a haircut?"
And I say,
"Yeah."
And they say,
"Oh, it looks nice."
And I say,
"Thanks."

You wanna know what I find fascinating about getting a haircut,
I am no longer a human being.
I am a piece of stone, and the barber is a sculptor.
He uses his razors as if they were chisels.
His hands move with the graceful confidence of a man who knows what he's doing.
I am just an uncarved block of sandstone, about to be transformed into a fresh figurine.

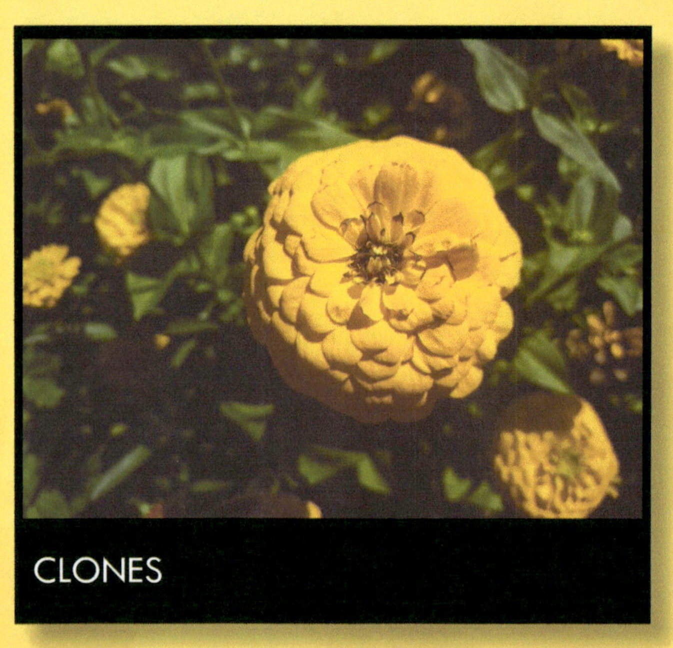

CLONES

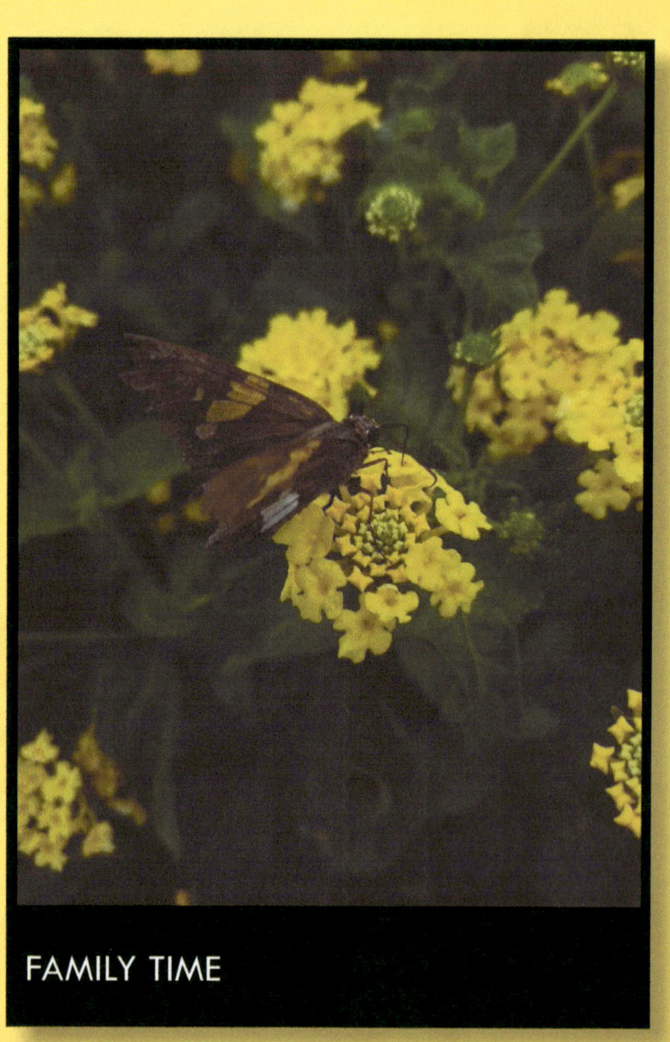

FAMILY TIME

Canary

Long days seem like endless nights.
The sky out of sight
Leaves only one source of light.
Lanterns tell which direction to go.
Light leads the way through icicles made of stone.
And it may lead the way home.

Although covered in grime and dust,
Although the constant movement wears them out,
They persevere with the little brawn they have left.

The rhythmic pounding of metal picks against stone
Matches the caged canary's song it sings.
But this graceful song doesn't last long.
The bright bird gives one last warning
Until its little lungs give in
There's something in the air
And it's not just the sound of the canary's last song
Which still lingers in the fog

Trees, cut down, turned into coarse tools.
Tools cut down stone and skin.
Causing rough calluses and piercing splinters
Cut skin, turned into strength.
Cut stone, already having it.

They're done.

Now, vacationing to the surface before another lifetime in the Underworld.
The turbulent ride to green and blue is long.
Some sit,
Some stand,
Some pace,
Some lean,
But none talk.

Sweat, dust, and oil
Churn together to create a morsel of vile flavors.
One now craving mum's apple pie.
Another wanting a savory steak.
And some longing for just a simple glass of water.

Finally,
The green and blue are here.
Like vampires, they've hidden from the light.
Greeted by the scent of fresh flowers.
An earthy fragrance fills the air with the passing rain.
They take a whiff and it smells like home.

Finally.
They're home,
Welcoming the sun,
Bright as a canary.

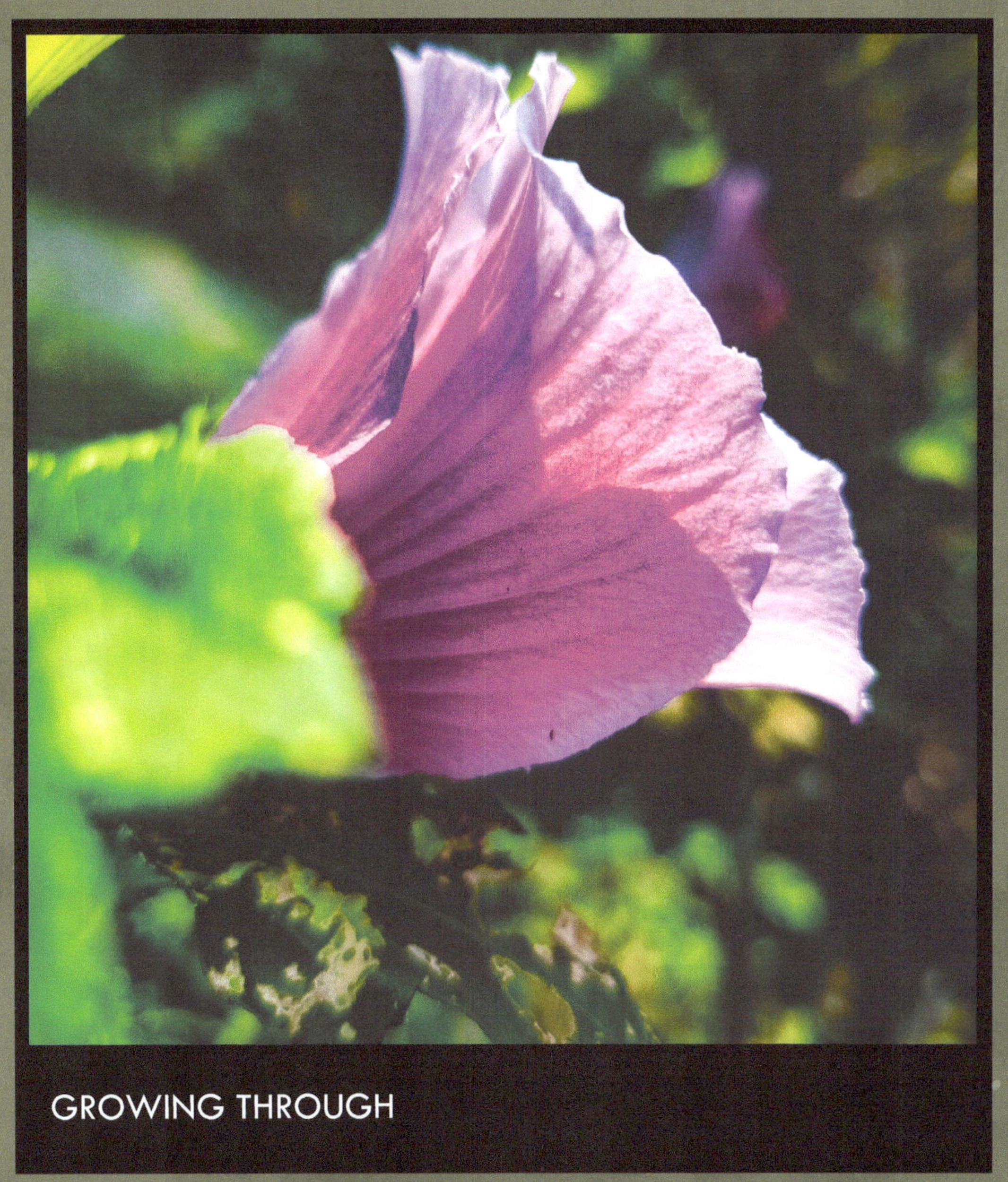

GROWING THROUGH

www.ingramcontent.com/pod-product-compliance
Lightning Source LLC
LaVergne TN
LVHW070222110826
845147LV00003B/623